Y0-DAC-551

Second

Worst

Joke Book

Dumb Jokes for Kids

By Steve Burt

Second Worst Joke Book

Dumb Jokes for Kids

By Steve Burt

ISBN-13: 978-1537762036
ISBN-10: 1537762036

Steven E. Burt
The Villages, FL 32162
352 391-8293

For my hilarious grandkids, Ben and Gracie Thomas, who love dumb jokes. The dumber, the better.

Dumb Jokes for Kids

1. How did the beaver get online?

He logged on.

2. What kind of car does Mickey Mouse's wife drive?

A minnie van.

3. What time does a tennis player get up?

Ten-ish

4. What do you call a deer with no eyes?
No i-deer.

5. What do you call a deer with no eyes and no legs?
Still, no i-deer.

6. What did the pirate say when he turned 80?
Aye Matey.

7. What do you get when you cross a stream and a brook?
Wet feet.

8. What's red and bad for your teeth?
A brick.

9. Why did the Jedi cross the road?

 To get to the Dark Side.

10. If you had 5 oranges in one hand and 5 pears in the other hand, what would you have?

The world's biggest hands.

11. Why do people work as bakers?

 They knead the dough.

12. What do you call Chewbacca when he has chocolate stuck in his hair?

Chocolate Chip Wookiee.

13. What clothes does a house wear?

Address.

14. Who makes more people smile than a clown?
A photographer.

15. Where are otters from?
Otter Space

Dumb Jokes for Kids

16. What did the duck say
when he bought lipstick?
Put it on my bill.

17. What did one elevator say to
the other?
I think I'm coming down with
something!

18. What does corn say when it
feels embarrassed?
"Aw, shucks!"

19. What did the little
mountain say to the big
mountain?
            Hi Cliff.

20. Why shouldn't you shower with Pokemon?
Because he might Pikachu.

21. What does a fish with no eye sound like?
Fsh, fsh, fsh.

22. Why wouldn't they let the butterfly into the dance?
It was a moth ball.

23. Where do cucumbers go on dates?
The salad bar.

24. What game do elephants play in a Volkswagen?
Squash.

25. What do you call  a bear with no teeth?
    A Gummy Bear.

26. How do you stop a snake from striking?
        Pay it decent wages.

27. What do you call a bear with no ear?
A b.

28. Why was the mushroom
invited to lots of parties?
He was a fungi to be with.

29. What does a dentist call his
x-rays?
Tooth-pics.

30. What did the buffalo say to
his son when he left for college?
Bison.

31. What do you give a dog for
a fever?

 Mustard, it's the best
thing for a hot dog.

32. What's worse than finding a worm in your apple?
Finding half a worm.

33. What do you call a cow with no legs?
Ground beef.

34. What do you call a camel with no humps?
Humphrey.

35. What stories do the ship captain's kids like best?
Ferry tales.

.

36. What do you get when you
pour hot water down a
rabbit hole?
Hot cross bunnies.

37. What letters
are not in the
alphabet?
The ones in the mail.

38. What time is it when an
elephant sits on your fence?
Time to get a new fence.

39. What vegetable is found in a basement?
Cellar-y.

 40. Why did the lion cross the road?
To get to the other pride.

41. What do you call a dog with no legs?
Doesn't matter, it won't come back anyway.

42. How can a leopard change its spots?
By moving.

43. Why did the crab cross the beach?
To get to the other tide.

44. Why does it take pirates so long to learn the alphabet?
Because they can spend years at "C".

45. What did the poodle say when it sat on the sandpaper?

Ruff.

46. Who went into the bear's cave and came out alive?
The bear.

47. Did you hear about the Italian chef who died?
Yeah, he pasta way.

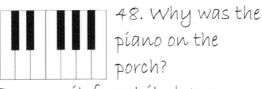

48. Why was the piano on the porch?
Because it forgot its keys.

49. What do ghosts like for dessert?
I scream.

50. Why don't eggs tell jokes?
They'd crack each other up.

51. What's black & white and eats like a horse?
A zebra.

52. Why did the orange stop at the top of the hill?
It ran out of juice.

53. Two waves had a race. Who won?
 Tide.

54. What is bright orange and sounds like a parrot?
A carrot.

55. What did one leaf say to another?
See you next fall.

56. Which vegetable can't you take on a boat?
Leeks.

57. Who has friends for lunch?
A cannibal.

58. Where did the king keep his armies?
In his sleevies.

 59. What did the digital clock say to it's dad?
Look pa, No hands.

2:00

60. What are the 3 greatest inventions to help people up in the world?
The elevator, the ladder and the alarm clock.

61. Which side of a chicken has the most feathers?
The outside.

62. What did the pony say when it had a sore throat?
I apologize, I am a little horse.

63. What do you call a boomerang that doesn't come back?
A stick

64. How do you communicate with a fish?
Drop him a line.

65. Why did the boy jump up and down before taking his medicine?
The label said:
Shake well before using!

66. What did the leopard say in the shower?
That really hits the spot.

67. What did one toilet say to the other toilet?
You look flushed.

68. What is a table you can eat?
A vegetable.

69. What is a tornado's
favorite game?
Twister!

70. Where do baby trees go to
school?
To a tree nursery.

71. Where were potatoes
first fried?
In Greece.

72. How do you repair a broken tomato?
Tomato Paste.

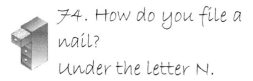

73. Where did the one-legged man work?
1-Hop.

74. How do you file a nail?
Under the letter N.

75. What pet is always found on the floor?
A carpet.

76. What is a kayaker's favorite kind of lettuce?
Row-maine.

 77. Where do apes sleep?
In APEricots.

78. Why did the man lose his job at the orange juice factory?
He couldn't concentrate.

79. What do you call a shoe made from a banana?
A Slipper.

 80. How many rubber ducks can you put in an empty bathtub?
One (after that it's not empty).

81. How do you catch a unique rabbit?
Unique up on it.

82. How do you catch a tame rabbit?
The tame way.

83. What happens when you throw a black cat in the Red Sea?
It gets wet.

84. How does Jack Frost travel?
By icicle.

85. Why did the scarecrow get a promotion?
He was outstanding in his field.

85. Why is History like a fruit cake?
Because it's full of dates!

86. What is a vampire's favorite food?
Neck-tarines.

87. Why did the banana go to the hospital?
Because it was not peeling well.

88. What did Cinderella say to the photographer?
When will I get my prints?

89. How long should a slipper be?
One foot.

90. Why do fish swim in salt water?
Pepper makes them sneeze.

91. What state has a friendly greeting for everyone?
Ohio.

92. What time is it when a clock strikes thirteen?
Time to fix the clock.

93. What would you call a beautiful cat?
A glamour puss.

94. What lights up a soccer stadium?
A soccer match

95. What foods are you able to can?
Cannibal food.

96. What did the mayonnaise say when someone opened the refrigerator door.
Close the door,
I'm dressing.

97. When's a chair like a fabric?
When it is satin.

98. What do you serve but never eat? A volleyball (or a tennis ball).

99. Why doesn't a bald man need any keys? Because he doesn't have any locks.

100. Why did Batman go to the pet shop? To buy a Robin.

101. What key opens a banana? A monkey.

102. Why did the chicken cross the basketball court?
The referee called foul.

103. What did the big chimney say to the small chimney?
You're too little to smoke.

104. What kind of apple isn't an apple?
A pineapple.

105. When is the moon heaviest?
When it's full.

 106. What does a crying baby ghost sound like?
"Boo-hoo! Boo-hoo!"

107. What do you call a song in a Subaru?
A cartoon.

108. How does a broom act on stage?
In sweeping gestures.

109. Why did the baker stop making donuts?
He got sick of the hole business.

110. What do you call a bear with no socks or shoes? Barefoot.

111. One is odd, 2 is even, 3 is odd, 4 is even. How do you make seven even? Take the s out.

112. Why were the suspenders sent to jail? For holding up the pants.

113. Were you long in the hospital?
No, I was the same size I am now.

114. Why did the rooster cross the road?
It was the chicken's day off.

115. What state has the smallest soft drinks?
Mini-Soda.

116. What bird is a letter?
A jay.

117. What's full of holes and still holds water?
A sponge?

118. How do you stop a charging bull?
Take away his credit card.

119. What did the porcupine say to the cactus?
Are you my mother?

120. Why is tennis so loud?
Players are always
raising a racket.

121. What bird do you hear at
mealtime?
A swallow.

122. What has a horn and gives
milk?
A milk truck.

123. Why is the letter "G"
scary?
It turns a host into a ghost.

124. What starts
with T, ends with T,
and is full of T?
A teapot.

125. Did you hear about the
magic tractor?
It went down the
road and turned
into a field.

126. Why did the elephant eat
the candle?
He wanted a light
snack!

127. What did the basketball
say to the baseball?
Nothing, it just
looked round.

128. What is at the end of
everything?
The letter G.

129. How do you keep your hair
dry in the shower?
Don't turn on the water.

130. Which cows chuckle?
Laughingstock.

131. Where do polar bears put their money?
In snow banks.

132. How does the teacher read schoolwork?
With her pupils.

133. What is the saddest bird?
A blue jay.

134. What is the most valuable fish?
Goldfish.

135. Why are some
fish at the bottom
of the ocean?
They dropped out of
school.

136. What do you get if you
cross a chicken and a poodle?
Pooched eggs.

138. What is a sleeping bag?
A nap sack.

139. Why do dogs wag their
tails?
Nobody else will   do
it for them.

140. What do wooden whales eat?
Plankton.

141. What kind of dog did the vampire have?
A bloodhound.

142. Did you hear about the wooden car with the wooden wheels and the wooden engine?
It wooden go.

143. What's a lifeguard's favorite game?
Pool.

144. Why was the baby ant so confused?
All of his uncles were ants.

145. What happened when the dog went to the flea circus?
He stole the show.

146. What do you call a chicken at the North Pole?
Lost.

147. How do you get a pig to a hospital?
Hambulance.

148. What do you get when you throw all the books in the world in the ocean?
A title wave.

149. What happened to the boy who drank 8 Cokes?
He burped 7-Up.

150. What runs but can't walk?
A faucet.

151. What runs but can't walk?
Your nose.

152. What is the science of shopping called?
Biology (buy-ology).

153. Where do cows go on a Saturday night?
To the moooovies.

154. What dog can jump higher than a building?
Any dog, buildings can't jump.

155. Why can't jungle animals take a test?
Too many cheetahs.

156. What is a bunny's favorite music?
Hip hop.

157. Why did the turtle cross the road?

 To get to a Shell Station!

158. Why do cowboys ride horses?
They're too heavy to carry.

159. Where did the horse go to get a new tail?
The Re-tail store!

160. A cowboy rode into town on Friday, stayed for 3 days then left on Friday. How did he do it?
His horse's name was Friday.

161. What lies at the bottom of the sea and shivers?
A nervous wreck.

162. What did Mickey Mouse say when Minnie Mouse asked if he was listening?
I'm all ears.

163. Why did the ram run over the cliff?
He didn't see the ewe turn.

164. Why were the apple and orange alone?
The banana split.

165. What is a zombie's least favorite room in the house?
The living room.

166. What do you call a retired vegetable?
A has-bean.

167. What is small, red and whispers?
A hoarse radish.

168. What do you do when your nose is on strike?
Picket.

169. What do you call a dancing sheep?
A baaaallarina.

 170. What comes after a monkey?
It's tail.

171. Why did the
chicken cross the
park?
To get to the other
slide.

 172. Why did the
skeleton go to the party
alone?
He had no body to go with him!

173. What is a navy officer's
favourite fruit?
Navel oranges.

174. When does the letter Z
come before the letter A?
In the word ZebrA.

175. What did the big bucket say to the little bucket?
You look a little pail.

176. What did the fly say when it flew into a window?
If I had more guts I'd do that again.

177. Did you hear about the guy who lost his left arm and leg in a car crash?
He's all right now.

178. Where do pencils come from?
Pencil-vania.

179. What is the difference between a bird and fly?
A bird can fly but a fly can't bird.

180. Where does Superman get the kind of food he needs to make him strong?
At the supermarket.

181. If you were in a candy shop and were about to die, what kind of candy would you get?

182. Why does the Mississippi river see so well?
Because it has four "i"'s.

183. Why do witches fly brooms?
Because vacuum cleaners are too heavy.

184. Why did the snail cross the road?
I'll tell you when he gets there.

185. How do fish go into business?
They start on a small scale.

186. Why did the one-handed man cross the road?
To get to the second hand shop.

187. If April showers bring mayflowers, what do mayflowers bring?
Pilgrims.

188. Why was Cinderella so bad at soccer?
She ran away from the ball.

189. What do you get when you cross a book with an egg??
A yolk book.
(The answer is not A DUMB JOKES FOR KIDS book.)

We hope you groaned and rolled your eyes at **Second Worst Joke Book**, the sequel to **First Worst Joke Book**, both in Steve Burt's **DUMB JOKES FOR KIDS** series. Look for **Third Worst** on Amazon in early 2017. For autographed and personalized copies, contact Steve by mail, by phone, or at one of his many book signings (New England summer & fall, Florida winter & spring).

Steve also writes the Mom's Choice Award-winning **FreeKs** psychic teen thrillers and the Bram Stoker Award-winning **Stories to Chill the Heart** books.

www.SteveBurtBooks.com
352 391-8293

Made in the USA
Middletown, DE
24 June 2019